THE
PEACH
SYMPHONY

Written & Composed by Christina Victoria

Copyright Page – The Peach Symphony

For permission requests, write to:
Marion Alexander Press
www.marionalexanderpress.com

Cover design by Christina Victoria
Published by **Marion Alexander Press**
Printed in the United States of America

ISBN: 9798218858940
LCCN: 2025925952
First Edition: 2025

The Peach Symphony | www.marionalexanderpress.com

Dedication

This is dedicated to the many versions of Me.

To the girl who danced on clouds like Tinkerbell,
light, unburdened, glowing without apology.

To the one whose heart lives deep near the ocean floor
a mermaid of sorts, breathing love where others could not.

To the woman who danced like nobody was watching,
the one who felt music in her bones before she understood herself.

To the woman who became a Mother.
The wife who learned.
The divorcée who rose.
The leader who carried entire teams on her back.
The friend who showed up even when her heart was breaking.
The woman who became her own light.

May you never forget these versions of you.
May you honor them all.

This is our encore. This is our opening night.

A celebration of the girl you were,
and the Woman you are constantly *becoming*...

Author's Note

This collection is a celebration of my evolution:

a devotion to the magic of my whimsical spirit,
a generational imprint whispered forward to my sons,
a love letter to my family and the rainbow-colored souls who orbit
my life,
a hymn honoring Black men and Black women in all their radiance,
and a tribute to love that endures, even when the world tries to
silence it.

Here, sensuality becomes language.
The woman becomes myth.
And the heart remembers itself.

If *Freedom Passage* was survival,
Peach Symphony is ascension.

Welcome to my world.
Welcome to music, the mystique
and my voice—exactly as it is.

~ *Christina Victoria*

An Invitation to The Symphony

Prelude to **The Peach Symphony**

Take a breath.
Fix your collar.
Smooth the silk along your waist.
Step into your softness.

The ushers are opening the doors.

Tonight, you are entering something more than a book.
More than poems.
More than pages stitched with ink and intention.

You… are stepping into a symphony.
My Symphony.

Your ticket?
That glow you brought with you.
That courage pressed against your ribs.
That knowing smirk you gave the mirror
before you walked out the door.

Look at you.
Finely dressed in confidence,
perfumed in purpose,
dripping in that quiet Southern elegance
that can't be taught.

Lipstick lined.
Edges laid or curls free.

Locs, coils, and silk press catching the light like a spotlight
whispering,

"Yes, honey. You. Center stage."

Your cologne is a bass line.
Your perfume is a high note.
Every step you take down this velvet aisle
is a rhythm all its own.

Welcome to **The Peach Symphony**.
Where the lights dim low,
the air sweetens,
and every chapter invites you deeper
into a world stitched with memory, melody, and magic.

This journey begins in **Duval.**
Heat and heartbeat.
Front porches humming with stories.
Summer thunder rolling through the air.
Childhood dancing bare feet and free.

It eases into **Charleston's** rose-kissed vineyards,
a lineage flavored with sweetness and survival.
Moss bending like prayer.
Generations of women moving with quiet fire.

It slides up through **D.C.'s** bass-thumping go-go,
A rhythm that grabs you by the waist
and teaches you a new way to breathe.

Then it drifts west into **Texas.**

Ingleside, Corpus Christi.
Where South Texas flavor meets Gulf Coast energy,
and warmth lingers like spice in the air.

Finally, it rises into **Atlanta**
the ***Black Mecca of the South.***
A modern Southern Renaissance,
where brilliance, culture, and rebirth
move like jazz in summer heat.

Here the senses overlap.

Sweet potatoes baked with brown sugar.
Seafood steaming fresh off a coastal dream.
BBQ smoke curling into the evening sky.
Fine wine uncorked with slow intention.
Molasses poured thick as memory.
Moonshine bold enough to loosen truth.
Chilled whiskey waiting at the juke joint,
where floorboards hum under tired feet
and the night always has one more story to tell.

Here, Love is eternal.
The heart sways like a melody you've always known.
Memory tastes like honey and smoke.
Longing lingers low
a saxophone at midnight.
Desire moves like jazz.
Improvised. Breathless. Unraveled.

Mornings rise in peach-colored light.
Nights fall soft as satin.
Music isn't just heard

It is felt.
In your chest.
In your hips.
In your lineage.

Every poem you are about to read
is a door.
A note.
A scene.
A memory resurrected
and a prayer poured forward.

And you belong here.
Right here.
In this theater of sound and story.

So come on in.

The house lights are lowering.
The conductor is lifting their hand.
The orchestra breathes.
The velvet curtains stir.

Take your seat, *Beloved.*

The **Peach Symphony**
is about to begin.

THE PEACH SUITE

PRELUDE: Moonlight & Sugar

Ethereal · Divine · Feminine

Moonlight & Sugar

Dressed in Honey

Scent of Summer

Miss Hummingbird

Whispers of a Fall Morning

Peach Goddezz

MOVEMENT I: When Horns Begin to Cry

Soulful· Cinematic · Reflective

When Horns Begin to Cry

Violins in the Sky

Morning Fog

Release

The Piano Knows My Name

Aquamarine Stanza

Duval Rhythm

The Peach Stanza

The Orchestra

The Open Sky

Mermaid in Minor Key: *Intermission*

MOVEMENT II: Becoming the Symphony

Sensual· Sacred · Self-Reclaimed

Sunrise in Silk

Into Eternity

Kissed in Peach

Peach Symphony (*title poem*)

Peach Prayer (*for Marion & Alexander*)

Lush Gardens

Let's Make Love on the Ocean Floor

Velvet Dusk: *Intermission*

ENCORE I: The Musicians

Magnetic· Mystical · Uninhibited

Bass Guitar

The Saxophone Player

Sill Caking

The R&B Singer

The Harp Seduction

Midnight Gospel

Trumpet Heart

The Opera Singer

The Cigar Bar

ENCORE II: The Lineage & The Legacy

Ancestral· Grounded · Triumphant

The Band Section

Helen's Song

Josie's Blues

Capricorn Rising

Sagittarius Dancer

Four Part Harmony

Emerald Frequency

Moonchild

Jade Couture: *Joy in the Heavens*

The Go-Go Band

Key Signature in Blue

ENCORE III: The Ether & The Echo

Soft· Incandescent · Otherworldly

Spirits that Travel

Jamaica Queens

Stardust

Echoes on the Leaves

Whiskey & Gardenias

When the Willow Swings

Black Velvet & Rose Gold

Marshmallow Clouds

The Rose Garden: *Intermission*

FINAL CURTAIN: Marion Alexander Cafe

Haitian· Charleston · Eternal

Where music settles, and legacy takes its seat.

Marion Alexander Café

Notes in Blue

Standing Ovation

CURTAIN CALL
The Women Crown in Light

FINAL BOW
The Conductor in Her Own Moonlight

HOUSE LIGHTS
A Benediction

PRELUDE: Moonlight & Sugar

Ethereal · Divine · Feminine

Moonlight & Sugar

The Moon found me half-awake,
stirring sweetness into my tea.
She slid through the blinds,
kissed the corner of my collarbone,
and whispered, "You've always been mine."

I didn't argue.
I just watched her light... *mesmerized* ...
spill over my hands like milk and mercy,
soft as a prelude played on quiet strings.

I used to call my softness fragile;
now I call it sacred.
I've learned the world will crave your sugar
then curse you for being sweet.
Still, I sweeten everything I touch
a slow-moving melody pouring from my palms.

She told me glow was a practice,
a discipline of tenderness.
That being gentle
isn't the same as being small.

I thought of every woman I've ever been
the one who gave,
the one who broke,
the one who learned to stay quiet
when her soul wanted to sing.

The one who laughed,
who danced a solo in the moonlight,
who found joy in little things
and the steady heartbeat of the earth.

And I thanked her.
All of them.
Because they made this version of me
honey-skinned, silver-lit,
pouring peace into my own cup
a whole orchestra warming up inside her chest.

Now, I glow.
Not because I am unbroken,
but because I've learned how to melt
and still shine.

The Moon and I…
we share the same language.
She sings, a low lunar lullaby,
and I rise in harmony.
Together,
we turn ordinary nights into hymns of light.

So, if you find me here, bathed in her gaze,
know this:
I am the sweetness I was always searching for.

Moonlight and **Sugar**
the opening note
of my return.

Dressed in Honey

I came gilded tonight
not guarded.
Every curve a confession,
every step its own soft hymn,
the quiet entrance music of a woman who knows.

The sun didn't rise
I did.
And she took notes
on how I glow.

Gold dripped slow across my shoulders,
thick with intention, like my hips
a warm alto sliding into the room
on a velvet tempo.
I am what warmth looks like
when it walks,
confident,
gliding like a black stallion set to its own rhythm.

They ask what I'm wearing.
"HONEY," I exclaim
and the whole room
sharpens its listening.

It's the scent of knowing.
Magnolias in the garden,
Gardenias in the sky
Southern bloom divine,
opening like the first note of a summer overture.

Time slows
when confidence enters the room.

Call me baby sugar
the taste of power
in patience.

Honeysuckle drips divinely from my lips,
in verse
and in sound.
My mouth speaks another language
part nectar,
part orchestra,
part promise.

I am poured, not painted
broad strokes across the midnight sky.
Sacred, not shy.
Soft enough to melt,
strong enough to stay whole
without breaking the rhythm.

Because this sweetness isn't borrowed.
It's built
with moonlight and sugar,
with the fragrance of summer and peaches,
with the warm pulse of a woman becoming.

Dripped from every dawn
I dressed myself in gold
and called it worship.

Every curve, a verse.
Every breath, a prayer of glow.

Every glance,
a quiet reminder:
this is what devotion looks like
when it finally learns
how to conduct its own light.

Scent of Summer

Bare shoulders, soft laugh,
a rhythm only the air remembers.
She walks like the hour after a storm
the kind that leaves everything glistening,
the kind that plays an adagio across the pavement.
Light trails her... lazy, golden, loyal
a warm brass section following at a distance.

The glint of perfume tracing her back,
a quiet rebellion against the breeze.
She smells of peaches and promise,
the kind of sweetness that knows its power,
the kind that enters a room like the opening chord of July.

Every step falls into worship:
gravel sighing, cicadas testifying,
Time itself hesitating
pausing the metronome of the day
just to catch another glimpse.

She doesn't chase summer.
She **is** the season
a pulse,
a fragrance,
a fever,
a whole symphony rising inside the heat.

And when she passes,
the air bows for her
every leaf, every light beam taking notes,

each one adjusting its pitch just to be near her.
Even the horizon blushes,
embarrassed by what she commands in her sway.

The world turns slow
soft, golden
drunk on her warmth,
like a deep Southern gospel humming through the dusk.

By the time she's gone,
the wind forgets its direction,
the dusk forgets its duty,
and everything smells
like her name.

Miss Hummingbird

The garden hums before she arrives.
Tuberose and jasmine bend in anticipation,
their perfume heavy with expectation
sweetness waiting to be witnessed.

Like magic
a flicker,
a glint of green spun in sunlight.

Miss Hummingbird drifts into view,
tiny body, vast command
a creature stitched from color
and quiet thunder.

Her wings, impossible
a thousand heartbeats
keeping time
with an unseen orchestra.

She doesn't rush.
She hovers
suspended between breath and belonging,
between the world that blooms
and the one that watches.

Every flutter becomes music.
Not the kind you hear
but the kind that makes air shimmer,
a soft tremolo vibrating through the leaves.

She dips her beak, soft, sure
into the mouth of jasmine,
sipping joy like scripture.

Never greedy.
Never still.
Just present
a tiny maestro conducting nectar and silence.

When she vanishes,
the garden sighs
as though beauty itself
just left the room,
leaving only the faintest echo
of her wing-born song.

Whispers of a Fall Morning

The morning met me like an old friend
soft, gold, and at ease.

A thin breath of fog curled along the edges of the yard,
settling itself gently over Georgia clay,
as though the earth was preparing
for something sacred—
the slow opening notes of day.

The air was crisp enough to wake me,
but tender enough not to rush me.

It held a hush
the kind that wraps around your shoulders
like a shawl woven from memory and grace,
the kind of quiet that feels like strings tuning
before the world begins its song.

Leaves whispered across the ground,
skittering like little messengers,
carrying secrets from places I used to be.

Somewhere in the distance, a bird called out
not loudly, not urgently
just a single soft note
to remind me that life continues,
even between beats.

I stood there barefoot on my porch,
feeling God in the cool wood beneath my feet,
feeling the universe settle itself into my lungs.

It was a moment made of stillness,
of golden light stretching itself
over the edges of my spirit
a slow, warm harmony reminding me
that softness
is also a form of strength.

And as the breeze moved through me,
it felt like the earth was saying,
in a gentle, familiar cadence,
"Here you are. Right on time."

Peach Goddezz: *A Juicy Reflection*

I'm the velvet peach
rising slow in golden light,
born from moonlight and Southern soil
a creature of warmth and wonder,
velvet-skinned and oceans-deep.

Too magical to bruise,
too seasoned to break,
held by a universe that cushioned my softness
and crowned my ripeness as truth.

What they see now
is power sharpened from tenderness,
a glow pulsing like prophecy.

I'm the curve that holds memory,
the mystical sway that makes poetry blush,
a delectable sweetness
that deepens with nearness,
awakening desire in those brave enough
to enter my gravitational field.

There are stars scattered in my laugh
and nectar thrumming in my pulse,
a fullness in my stride,
my heels playing their own rhythm
strong and commanding,
with 10,000 orchestras rising behind me.

Each step whispers abundance,
no more apologies.

I am a music sheet divine,
edges weathered but consecrated
sacred
because I healed.
Powerful
because I grew into a woman
who remembers her own magic.

Deep, rich coffee on a dewy Southern morning,
the kind that warms your chest before the sun fully wakes.

I'm the bubbly champagne poured beneath magnolia blooms,
bubbling light against dark petals,
effervescent as a whispered promise.

Cool whiskey sour brushing your lips
on a wet summer night
that slow, smoky sweetness
that lingers on the tongue
long after touch has disappeared.

I am taste and temptation,
ritual and desire,
a flavor carved from moonlight and fire.

The mermaid queen
ruler of emotion,
the woman who feels in colors,
who catches feelings the way others catch rain
gently, deeply, without fear.

Often fantasized about, quietly,
in purple rooms of blue magic

a statuesque goddess before her time,
whose spirit has kissed the earth,
soul-deep for a million miles.

Deep brown eyes of mystery and calm,
full of stories never told.

Melodies that rise like prayer,
chords echoing through the mountains
old, ancestral, trembling in the bones
and keys played on the moon

Who is she?

The woman whose laughter tastes like summer,
whose walk summons storms and sunlight,
her presence makes quiet rooms sit up straighter.

The one whose hips remember ancient drumbeats,
whose breath cradles galaxies,
whose softness could heal a man
and whose boundaries could save herself.

Tell the world: Peach Goddezz.

She's not just composed
She's devoured. Savored.
She's divine.

She's Me. Juicy. Eternal.

A whole symphony walking in skin
a masterpiece that keeps unfolding…

MOVEMENT I: Horns Begin to Cry

Soulful· Cinematic · Reflective

When Horns Begin to Cry

The stage hums before she appears.
A velvet hush
every heartbeat holding its place.

Carnegie Hall smells of perfume and fear,
of cigars and applause not yet earned.
A gardenia wilts against her hair,
its petals surrendering to the heat,
but the bloom stays — proud, perfumed, trembling.

A white gown draped in ache and satin,
gloves climbing her wrists like prayer.
A glimmer at her throat; small, defiant,
catching the light she never asked for.

The band waits.
Trumpet polished, drum poised,
saxophone warm against someone's chest.
They know who she is
the woman who made the night itself
fall to its knees.

She steps forward,
carrying everything and nothing.
No armor. No disguise.
Just a flower, a glow,
and the weight of a thousand whispers.

When the horns begin to cry,
the air turns honey and smoke.

Her voice
raw silk, frayed at the edges,
sweet with the ache of survival.

Each note drips slow
molasses and memory.

You can taste the rooms that never loved her back,
the men who mistook her glow for weakness.
You can hear the hunger in her vowels,
the tremor of withdrawal in her sighs,
And still, she sings.

The band follows her like prayer.
The trumpet bends to her ache,
the bass anchors beneath her grief,
and the sax
weeps in time with her breath.

She closes her eyes,
and for a moment, she's gone
not lost, but free.
Every ghost she's ever carried
now sits in the front row,
listening…

That song.
The one she had to fight to sing.
The one the world tried to silence.

Her lips part,
and Strange Fruit spills into the air
slow, sacred, unforgiving.

No one coughs.
No one dares.
And the chandeliers tremble.

It's not music anymore
it's protest.
It's prayer.
It's proof.

When the horns begin to cry,
it isn't sorrow
it's surrender.
It's the sound of survival
finally exhaling.

The final note lands like grace.
The gardenia droops lower,
a single petal falling onto her glove
white against the tremble of her pulse.

The crowd rises.
Applause thunders like absolution,
but she only bows once,
eyes half-closed,
as if she already knows
the night didn't save her.
She saved the night.

for Billie, in this imagined moment where she taught the world to ache in key.

Violins in the Sky

Some nights,
the air remembers me.
It breathes my name like promise
low, golden, unbothered.

The moon shifts on her throne,
and somewhere above the clouds,
a thousand violins lift their bows
ready to play
what only I can feel.

I tilt my head and listen.
The stars tremble on cue,
the sky opens like a stage,
and I take my place
barefoot, breathless,
crowned in calm.

The first note cuts through the night,
soft as perfume,
sharp as power.
It isn't sorrow
it's declaration.

The air bends around me.
My body becomes instrument
hips the tempo,
spine the measure,
pulse the percussion
that calls the light closer.

The world stops
to watch me rise.
No ache.
No aftermath.
Only radiance
pure, deliberate, undeniable.

I move like a hymn
remixed by heaven.
Each step a chord,
each sigh a symphony,
each glance a note sustained.

Because tonight,
I am the music and the miracle
the muse and the maestro,
the crescendo and the calm.

And somewhere above this moment,
the violins in the sky
play…
just for me.

Morning Fog

In the dewy garden of the morning fog,
there she sits, uninhibited,
as the sun begins its slow return
and catches the soft, silhouetted glow
of her body.

The fog curls around her like memory,
a veil that both reveals and hides
the kind of beauty you admire
but approach carefully,
like a muted horn warming in the distance.

The dew gathers on the grass,
slipping down each blade
as though greeting her arrival,
it recognizes her spirit
before you ever speak her name.

Pecan skin unapologetic.
Legs thickly crossed at her thighs.
The juiciness of her lips and hips
settling into the luxury of her garden chair.

Gold stilettos nestled close by
witnesses, not ornaments
silent as cymbals before the strike.

Her spirit floats into the dawn of time,
laughter echoing only in memory,
conversations drifting through the air
secrets buried deep,

locked in the quiet chambers
of the earth's forgiving core.

Descended, yet the fog knows her.
It holds her shape in its drifting edges,
keeps her laughter suspended in its hush,
as her spirit moves between dawn and memory
like a soft refrain returning home.

An addict of love, of attention, of life.
An indescribable beauty
who returned to the soil and the sky.

Her conversations still travel
through the morning air
whispers draped in fog,
notes carried low,
secrets locked deep in the earth's warm core.

She was complicated, vexed
beautiful in the way fog is beautiful:
soft if you behold it,
dangerous if you dare not understand it.

Her presence still lingers
cool against the skin,
warm in the bone
a quiet music on the edges
of where morning becomes memory.

Release

You've been holding
for far too long

years of neglect and disappointment,
romantic starvation,
being unprotected,
carrying everything alone,
loving without being met,
pretending you were okay
in a world that kept asking you to be strong.

And for the first time in a very long time…

Someone took care of you.
Held you.
Saw you.
Protected you without being asked.
Chose you with intention,
not convenience.

And your body
your soft, tired, sacred body
didn't know what to do
with that kind of honest, grown-man love…
so it let go.

The cry wasn't grief.
It wasn't loss.
It wasn't fear.

It was your heart unclenching,
your spirit unburdening

a quiet horn note trembling in your chest,
vibrating through years of silence.

It was your ribs widening,
your breath returning to itself,
your pulse settling into a rhythm
that finally felt like safety.

It was your soul whispering:
"Oh my God…
this is what it feels like to be loved."

And in your strength,
in your brilliance,
and in all the worlds you carry

You are still human.
Still allowed to soften.
Still allowed to feel.

So, breathe.
Loosen.
Let yourself rise
on this new, steady melody.

Release.

The Piano Knows My Name
When the Air Turns to Fire:

The night smelled like champagne and rhythm.
Soft brass in the corner, voices melting into smoke.
I moved through the crowd like a secret,
skin glimmering under the hush of candlelight.
each step its own quiet gospel.

The lights dimmed lower.
And there he was
sitting at the piano,
fingers dressed in light.
Cool. Steady. Handsome enough
to make the air forget its name.

He played something slow,
a melody that leaned into the room
and undressed the silence.
My pulse followed the rhythm,
hips swaying before permission,
drawn toward him like smoke to flame.

I didn't know his name,
but my soul swore it did.
It stirred in my chest
a recognition older than memory,
the past exhaling.

Another glance,
and time bent its knees.
I moved closer
breathing in the space between notes,

hearing everything he wasn't saying.

His hands spoke in a language older than us both,
every chord a confession,
every pause a pulse of skin on skin.

He played like he'd been waiting
as if I were the missing key,
he could never reach
until I walked in.

When our eyes met,
something ancient uncoiled.
He smiled
that slow, knowing smile
of a man who already knows the ending.
And somewhere between treble and bass,
our hearts shook hands and stayed there.

Years would pass
oceans, distance, silence.
Yet the piano remembers my name.
No matter who sits at the keys,
it finds its way back to that night …
to us.

I've heard other songs since,
beautiful ones
but none that felt like home.

Because even now,
when music fills the room,
I feel him still playing for me

his rhythm running through my veins,
my name lingering between his notes.

He doesn't have to be here.
The melody is.

And somewhere, beneath candlelight and chords,
the piano still calls me back
to the night *When the Air Turns to Fire*.

Aquamarine Stanza

She wrote her heart in water,
ink dissolving into tide.
Each word a secret shimmer,
each sigh a promise.

The sea caught her rhythm gently,
rocked her pain into a song,
made her grief sing hallelujah,
turned her solitude to strong.

Waves rose to memorize her shape,
currents carried her prayer through coral;
every ripple spoke her story softly,
every breath became immortal.

Ships passed by, blind to the language
unfolding beneath their gleaming beams
a woman born of melody and moon,
keeper of the ocean's dreams.

The moon bent low to listen closely,
spilling light across her skin
each droplet crowned her temple sweetly,
each shimmer called her kin.

She wore Aquamarine like the night,
a gorgeous crown of mystic power,
stars woven in her light.

And when the deep remembered her name,
it echoed through blue cathedral halls

soundwaves bowing at her ankles,
saltwater rising just to touch her.

She did not break beneath the pressure;
she bloomed.

A quiet blaze in turquoise darkness,
a hymn cupped in the ocean's palms.

Now she lives beneath the surface,
half-song, half-sacred lore
the ocean's favorite stanza,
the tide's eternal encore.

Duval Rhythm

For the Jacksons and the streets that sang me home.

The first sound was bass.
Boom of a car rolling down 6th and Fairfax,
windows rattling,
air thick with heat and honey.

Somebody yelling, "DUUUVALLL!"
and the block answering back in harmony.

The city was alive
hot grease popping from Jenkins BBQ,
saxophone slipping out of Jim's Place,
church bells and basslines arguing about salvation.

Every street corner had its own choir:
State. Ernest. Lewis. Morgan.
Four notes in the gospel of home.

We were born on rhythm
our Grandmas shouting Hallelujah
with tambourines that knew
heartache and joy.

Our mamas moved like Sunday dresses,
hips swaying to Al Green and Anita Baker,
voices carrying across porches
like secrets wrapped in smoke.

We danced before we could crawl,
stomped before we could pray.

Our laughter shook like brass
sweet, loud, unapologetic.

We had crab boils on the curb,
boomboxes baptizing the air,
and Mary Ann's Fried Chicken
tasting like it had been touched by God himself.

Friday nights:
ribs and rhythm,
blue lights and gold smiles.
Jim's Place. Jazz Co. The Post.

We dressed like the world was watching,
and it was.
Downtown glowed electric.

The Landing sang back to the river,
and the wind carried the hum of history
marches, love stories,
names whispered in the brick.

You could feel the past moving through your bones,
the way the saints turned the struggle into sound.

From Georgia roots to Duval bloom,
we made music out of everything
loss, laughter, Sunday rain,
the way we kept surviving in rhythm.

I was raised on that sound
the rush of the water hose,
the hiss of a hot comb,
the bass of men laughing outside the corner store.

Every note a memory.
Every beat, a prayer.

So when I say "Duval,"
I mean holy ground with hoop earrings.
Ribs, rhythm, and the neighborhood resilience.
People who could make harmony out of heartbreak,
and still find a reason to two-step in the parking lot.

That's where I'm from.
That's who raised me.

DUVAL …

the rhythm in my blood,
the song that made me.

The Peach Stanza

They call me Stanza
because every line of me sings.

Every curve, a pause.
Every breath, a break.
My body speaks in enjambment,
rolling from word to word
without apology.

I am the verse the poets chase,
the peach that bruises beautifully
soft on the outside,
but filled with a rhythm
that can make a man forget his name.

Taste me once
and you'll hear the vowels round,
the consonants melt.

I speak in languages older than touch
murmurs of honey,
syllables of silk.

I don't rhyme.
I rise.
I don't wait to be written.
I write myself.

My skin glows like metaphors at midnight.
My hips keep the beat of poems unborn.
Even silence listens when I move.

Because I am not just stanza

I am Sermon.
I am Spell.
I am the soft punctuation between Lust and Light.

And when you read me,
and your lips brush my name,
you'll understand
this isn't poetry.

It's worship.

The Orchestra

They didn't arrive as strangers
they drifted in as sound,
as rhythm,
as color,
as the early trembling notes
of the woman I was tuning myself to become.

They were the first music
my spirit learned by heart.

Before language,
before love,
I knew *them*...

The girls who rose beside me
from Brookview to Sandalwood,
through Jheri curls at Miss Jimmie's,
and talent-show performances.

Chorus-room echoes,
through prom-night glitter.
heartbreak's first bruise,
seven-year-old secrets
and seventeen-year-old flight.

Their laughter cracked open the sky.
Loyalty stitched my edges.
Their rhythm still moves
in the quieter rooms of my heart.

A garden of color and culture,
women who turned sidewalks
into stages,
pain into something
we survived together.

Wind chimes in the heat.
Tambourines in the dark.
A drumline steadying the hands
of a girl holding too much world
too soon.

Some women love you as you are.
These women loved me
before I knew the shape
of who that was.

From the tall Laura Street building
overlooking the Landing
where we dreamed big,
laughed louder,
and grew in different directions
while staying stitched at the soul
they became the harmony
I never outgrew.

The DMV called my name
Go-Go drumbeats pounding
through brick and bone,
music that rearranged your spirit
without asking permission.
Those women… whew.
Grown Woman energy.

They taught me to walk like midnight royalty,
to wear my curves like prophecy,
to hold myself
like every version of woman
was already living in my bones.

Bassline spirits.
Hi-hat laughter.
Love that stayed
after the last note faded.

Texas wrapped me in warmth
spice, softness,
fire tucked beneath tenderness.

Women who held me in their culture,
loved me in ways that made distance
feel small
and belonging
feel like home.

Their instrument was guitar
slow-strummed, amber-warm, sun-kissed.
A sweetness that lingered
off the Gulf Coast.

When I returned
to Duval soil,
there were women
in the cosmetics temples
of MAC and CHANEL.

Women who dusted magic

onto my skin,
and reminded me I was light
before I remembered it myself.

From my love of beauty
to the birth of Christina Victoria Cosmetics,
you showed up with hands and heart
packing shine,
painting dreams,
turning lip gloss and mascara
into belief.

You planned.
You lifted.
You gathered the light
and helped me offer it back to the world.
I adore you.

Corporate brought me Wonder Woman
a woman carved in kindness and clarity,
who stepped into my life by chance
and stayed on purpose,
her love for my journey
and my family
woven deep into my soul.

Atlanta was where
the whole Orchestra rose up again
a glittering, breathing composition
of women who met me like destiny.

Philly's edge,
Brooklyn fire,

Panamanian humor,
down-south soul,
Gary, Indiana grit
women already rehearsing my arrival
before I walked in the door.

Brass brilliance.
Golden confidence.
The grounding and the lift.
The reminder and the revelation.

They sharpened me.
Softened me.
Held me.

Their love
a full chorus,
loud, layered, alive.

When I look at them
Duval, DC, Texas, Atlanta
I see an Orchestra of women
who refused to let me go silent.

My strings and percussion.
My brass and my wind.

They did not make me perfect.
They made me possible.
They tuned my universe.

Shaped my edges.
Lifted the roof off my sky
and called me
Friend, Sister, Heart, Home.

And somewhere in that sacred noise
all those cities,
all those years,
all that laughter,
all that survival

I became music.
Because every symphony begins
with a woman loved loudly
by the right ones.

And I was.
I Am.

Forever conducted
by the Orchestra
of Women
who made me.

The Open Sky

He wasn't tall,
but his presence stretched wide
like the open sky after rain,
or a guitar chord held long enough
to settle in your chest.

He spoke in music,
midnight melodies sent without warning,
the kind a man only releases
when he's stripped of pretense
and full of truth.

There was a softness in how he saw me
not as a woman passing through,
but as a verse worth lingering on,
a harmony worth returning to.

We weren't a story,
not really.
But we were a spark,
a rest note,
a warm intersection
of timing and intention.

And though the road took us
in different directions,
I keep a piece of that open sky
from Tampa to Georgia
the one he carried in his voice,

in his laughter,
in the quiet rhythm
that made me feel seen
in the simplest of ways.

INTERMISSION I —*Mermaid in Minor Key*

Mermaid in a Minor Key: *Intermission*

There is a cognac in their voice
a low, amber chord
that lingers against her skin.
She craves and adores it,
while it pours through her like a warm, slow brass line.

And when they blush
that boyish grin,
and breathless little giggle...
it's a soft cymbal kiss in the dark,
a moment that wakes the music in her bones.

So, she entertains.
Teases and she flirts.

She becomes the melody they follow into deeper waters,
never the harmony they can hold.

The uninhibited goddess in disguise
a spirit slipping through their sheets after midnight,
the dew resting on the grass
as the sun takes its final bow.

She likes to make them blush,
to tilt the rhythm,
to shift the tempo with a single line.

She knows the notes that pull them forward,
the cadence that unravels them,
the current that makes the tide rise.

She might be good for you,
good to you ...
but she is nothing you should ever confuse as need.

Tread carefully. Move with intention.

She is the mermaid in a minor key,
the solo you chase but never catch
the haunting melody
that draws you close with moonlit hands
and releases you with a smile
back into your shallow water.

A sweet danger.
A beautiful warning.
A score you cannot keep.

MOVEMENT II: Becoming the Symphony

Sensual· Sacred · Self-Reclaimed

Sunrise in Silk

The room is still vibrating from the night before,
sunlight painting hymns across the shadows of the wall.
Satin drapes off her voluptuous frame,
her skin glowing iridescently, soft as silk.

She stretches, slow, certain
a woman reborn in peach light.

The air tastes like mangoes and promise.

Her perfume drifts, a quiet encore
from skin that remembers every note of touch,
every sigh that became prayer.
No audience this time.
No need to perform.

Just her breath and stillness,
a soft metronome between heartbeat and hallelujah.
The city is still half-asleep,
but she rises, deliberate,
pulling the day onto her shoulders like a robe.

She moves toward the edge of the bed,
her feet brushing the wooden floor
soft, gentle, cold to the touch.

Her right ankle glints in gold.
Her hips sway softly, humming low jazz.
She passes the long mirror;
her reflection winks back in rhythm.

This is not awakening.
It is continuation
the big band still playing softly in the morning sky,
the same one that roared the night before.

The air still holds,
a slow burn carried into daylight.
She pours herself morning gold,
sipping slowly, careful not to burn her lips.

Her movement is a melody of ease,
each step a declaration of presence.

And as the tall windows catch the sunlight on her collarbone,
a voice in the faint distance whispers, *"Good morning."*

Tender. Soft. Commanding. Secure.
She smiles.
Because this is what divine femininity looks like
flesh and silk,
unapologetic,
Alive!

Into Eternity

He's beautiful
because of how he loves me
unwavering,
unapologetic.

In the way he sees me,
chooses me,
holds me like a song,
and kisses me
into eternity
slow, tender,
as though his mouth
is composing forever
against mine.

Kissed in Peach

There were kisses on my shoulders,
measured, certain
the kind that know exactly where to land,
like notes placed with intention
on warm, waiting skin.

They traveled down the line of my back,
slow as warm honey,
soft as a promise whispered into a melody
only my body could hear.

It was lush,
it was juicy
a sweetness that opened me,
a quiet symphony rising in my chest,
reminding me that my body remembers
every soft place
where pleasure once lived.

A moment I could taste again
if I closed my eyes long enough
peach-sweet,
honey-warm,
a lingering chord
still humming along my spine.

Peach Symphony

They call me **Peaches.**
Born from moonlight and sugar,
enough to tempt the gods.

Sweetness that stains your memory,
that lingers on your fingertips
long after the touch.

My touch leaves echoes
the scent of summer on your hands.

I'm sunrise dressed in honey,
the hush between heartbeat and breath,
glowing even when the sun forgets to look.

But another called me **Symphony.**

Because of my sound
the way my heels danced across midnight sidewalks,
clicks and echoes marking time like jazz.

Rhythm in my walk,
the whisper between my thighs as they brushed together,
making music that could tempt
the most disciplined soul.

I am movement.
Crescendo.
The trumpet that wakes the sky,
the violin that whispers to the moon,

the steady drum that lives in the heart
of every man who's ever tried to love me.

Symphony is the language my spirit speaks
when words fail
the way my bones hum
in the black night sky.

So what happens
when sweetness meets sound,
and the air turns to fire?

When the soft fruit meets the roaring horn section,
and I rise.

Depending on the moon,
call me **Peaches**
the softness you taste,
the glow you crave.

Or call me **Symphony**
the song that lifts you higher,
opening you to the ballet, the dance,
the ache of remembering beauty.

I am both.

The taste and the tune.
The fruit and the flame.
The glow and the sound
that refuses to fade.

I am the echo you feel
long after I'm gone,
the hymn your heart plays
when the night remembers me.

Peach Prayer for Alexander & Marion

There is a rhythm that runs through our blood,
older than the house I built,
older than my own becoming.

It began with a man in Charleston
who planted roses that still bloom when it rains,
and a woman whose hands carried the scent of soil and prayer.

Their song found me.
And through me, it found you.

You, my suns
Marion's name reborn in your laughter,
Alexander's strength pulsing in your dreams.

You are the echo of every man who loved without words,
and every woman who survived by remembering how to sing.

I prayed for peace once,
and God sent me light in duplicate.

Two stars rising from the same sky,
pulling my heart in equal, magnetic directions.

You remind me that legacy is not marble or money
it's the way your laughter warms a room,
the way your silence stills the air.
It's the way you carry my father's wisdom
and your grandmother's defiance
without knowing you do.

If ever the world grows heavy,
remember
you come from a line of dreamers and fighters,
gardeners and poets,
men who built homes from dust
and women who called that dust sacred.

I look at you now
and see generations answered.

The prayer that began before my breath
has your names stitched inside it.

And when I am gone
when my voice is memory
and my glow fades into morning
know that you were the song I sang the longest,
the melody that kept the world turning.

You are my peach prayer
my offering,
my sunrise,
my continuation of love.

The promise whispered through generations,
the hallelujah carried in our name.

You are every answered prayer
my grandmother never got to say,
and every new beginning
my father dreamed into motion.

When the wind moves through the magnolias,
know that it is me
reminding you that love outlives the body,
that light never forgets its source.

And when the world grows quiet,
listen.

You'll hear me humming in your laughter,
soft and endless,
a peach prayer
still rising.

~ *Mom*

Lush Gardens

The night breathes low
cicadas playing backup
to the slow spin of a record.
The moon leans in close,
watching us like it's jealous.

You say my name
and it spills from your tongue like honey.
Somewhere between your smile
and my slow inhale,
the air thickens with *maybe*.

Your hand grazes mine
Brief. Electric.
a promise posing as an accident.

The garden listens,
The magnolias hold their breath.

You shift closer,
close enough for me to feel your rhythm
without a word crossing the space between us.

I catch the bassline of your heart,
the song we're about to play.

The scent of peach and bourbon
drifts through the night,
and I can't tell if it's from your skin
or the glass.

Either way,
I'm *intoxicated.*

The world slows to a hush.
Your thumb grazes my lip
a note waiting to be sung.

I want to tell you
I don't need a chorus,
that this duet is enough.

But instead,
I breathe you in.
Soft. Deliberate.
Letting the silence
say everything.

Because here,
under moon and jasmine,
we don't fall in love.

We **bloom** in it.
Slowly.
Fully.

Like two vines
learning the shape
 of each other.

Let's Make Love on the Ocean Floor

Let's make love on the ocean floor
where sound slows
and the waves hold their breath.

Your hair floats like song,
a symphony of beautiful coils
dancing with the tide.

Me on top,
weightless in your orbit,
our rhythm matching
the hush between heartbeats and sea foam.

The current moves around us
a melody older than our names.
I feel safe inside your gravity,
suspended in something true.

You, chocolate drifting in blue.
Me, sunlight in gold surrender.
We move as prayer,
as pulse,
as sound turned human.

Your eyes say everything.
Notes unplayed.
Verses unspoken.
We dissolve into rhythm,
tide and body,
one.

And when we rise
skin glistening like new dawn,
our fingers almost touch the surface.

The sea sings your name.
The light breaks.
You disappear into air

Just water,
Just sound,
Just memory.

And the ocean keeps our secret.
A love that was never touched by land,
but lives beneath the surface,
long after the moon has turned away.

INTERMISSION II — Velvet Dusk

Velvet Dusk *Intermission*

The room doesn't go quiet
it softens
into a low, settling note.

The sky quietly roars above me
as the moon makes its entrance through the bay windows,
a silver overture gliding across glass,
slow and deliberate,
like the first bowed string of night.

Light leans low against the walls,
gold thinning into amber,
as the day loosens its grip
and the tempo drops
without announcement.

Something sacred slips
between the measures of my breath
not the hush of an ending,
but that long-held rest
before the next movement begins.

Skin remembers the warmth
of the previous song.
Air holds sweetness
in its undertone.
But now the rhythm rounds itself,
slows into intention.

This is the moment
after the crescendo

when presence takes over.
The glow no longer searches
it sustains.
The heart no longer reaches
it knows.

Velvet dusk...
where heat dims into harmony,

The night trades silk for reverence,
and the music prepares
to be witnessed
instead of chased.

ENCORE I: The Musicians

Magnetic · Mystical · Uninhibited

Bass Guitar

You didn't touch me first.
You tuned me.

Found the G string of my breath,
the A string of my wanting,
brushed the low E of my hunger,
checking the tension
of something sacred.

You slid through frets
as though each one held
a remembered version of me
1st for curiosity,
3rd for recognition,
5th for the shift in my breathing
when I realized you'd heard something
I wasn't saying.

Your fingers learned my quiet
before they ever touched my skin
mapping the 7th fret of my softness,
the 9th of my ache,
the 12th where sound
stops pretending to be sound
and becomes pulse.

You played me
without rushing the progression,
letting each note bloom slow,
as though the universe leaned in
to listen to you explore me.

And when your thumb settled
on the octave of my longing,
I swear the night bowed its head
just to honor the moment.

You didn't need a lyric.
You didn't need a cue.

You found the chord in me
that had been waiting
for a musician of spirit,
not ego.

Somewhere between your inhale
and the warmth of your nearness,
my body opened like a full-moon tide
quiet, inevitable,
drawn to the gravity of your knowing.

You touched me
like the bassline of a galaxy
steady, inevitable,
the kind of sound that rearranges bone,
the kind that teaches a woman
she is not made of skin alone.

You leaned in closer,
and suddenly the room was gone.
The air, gone.
The walls, gone.

Only vibrations remained.

You pressed the 15th fret
 of my surrender,
and the universe tuned itself
to the pitch of my breath.

Quietly.
Reverently.
You played the part of me
that had forgotten
it was still living.

My spirit left first
eager, weightless, remembering.
Then my body followed,
soft, willing, unguarded,
like a hymn that knew
it would be caught.

We rose through something
no language explains,
a place beyond touch,
beyond sight,
beyond the shape of our own names.

We met
not in a bed,
not in the night,
but somewhere between planets,
where sound becomes color,
and color becomes heat,
and heat becomes prayer.

You found me there
the stardust version of myself,
the one I only become
when someone plays me
with intention.

You understood
that pleasure is a form of reverence,
because you knew
a woman like me
is a whole instrument
to be honored,
not consumed.

As morning softened the sky,
the bassline lingered beneath my ribs,
a slow, golden hum
that followed me into waking,
reminding me of one truth:

I was not undone.
I was remembered.

And the music
is still playing
where you tuned me last.

The Saxophone Player

We sat there in the juke joint,
anticipation thick as smoke.

Laughter spilled between whiskey glasses,
our lips catching the starlight, slick, ready.

The air from the river carried notes of night,
and perfume we couldn't quite name.

The room waited.
Suspended.
And there he was.

Tall. Dark. Incredibly handsome,
like someone stole his face from the love gods.
Unbothered. Certain.
Moving with that quiet grace
only men who know themselves possess.

He stepped to the mic,
and the floorboards fell silent.

He smiled.
Slow. Electric.
His teeth lighting the crowd
a smile that rearranged the room.
And just like that,
he owned every heartbeat in the room.

He pressed his lips to the brass,
slow, certain

and the air filled with Grover Washington Jr.
a tone so smooth
it made the darkness blush.

The room went still…
Even the wind forgot its name.

His fingers, long and deliberate,
stirred something I'd buried in silk.
Each breath became a confession,
a rhythm across my skin.

He bent each note like a promise,
rolled his wrists in forgiveness.
Sound spilled over his collarbone,
into the shadows between my ribs,
and I swore I felt him
not beside me,
but inside me
somewhere between ache and the exhale.

I tried not to stare.
Failed completely.

My mouth open,
caught mid-hallelujah.

He looked up once.
And I swear,
he saw me
before the note left his lungs.

The lights dimmed deeper

amber and smoke curling around his crown,
a halo for the man who'd kissed God
and brought the sound back with him.
The audience swayed,
souls tethered to his tempo
breathing when he breathed,
breaking when he did.

Every sigh of that horn
touched something tender in me.

And when he stopped
when silence fell like a curtain,
I could still hear him playing
somewhere inside my bones.

My spirit rose,
floating freely into the universe,
carrying the echo of his sound
a hymn, a haunt,
a melody too sacred to name.

Still Caking

She was a stallion long before the world
tested her cadence
hips carved like God was composing curves,
breasts sitting like whispered rumors,
legs shaped for any stage she chose.
Five-three,
but she moved like a skyline rising
a slow crescendo,
a woman whose footsteps could set an overture in motion.

Back then,
we were twenty-something and wildfire,
leaving sweat on the floors of Jim's Place and The Post,
spinning the night into our own private soundtrack.

She spit Lil' Kim and Remy Ma like verses were oxygen,
bars slicing through the bassline
as if the world needed to hear her announce herself.

And TRUST
she wore her crown with an ease
that made Queens look twice.

She cooked like the ancestors stirred the pot beside her,
season and spirit in every dish.
She worked three jobs like she was triple-blessed,
moved through the week with a hustler's heartbeat.

"Still Caking" wasn't just her brand.
It was the melody she lived by
before branding had a name.

Her sewing machine sang midnight solos,
turning her wedding dress
into a runway proclamation
thread and vision in perfect harmony.

She never needed permission to be magic;
she conjured beauty the way musicians breathe:
effortless, necessary, divine.

And when life shifted the key,
her pecan skin still held its glow,
those expressive eyes still carried firelight,
those juicy lips still curved like truth
soft but certain.

That's the Queen I know
stitched with grit,
draped in grace,
a Virgo who delivered truth in clean, sharp notes,
and a Pisces who received it
like water meeting the shore.

We have clashed,
paused,
and returned
because our friendship is a song with too much history
to ever go quiet.

Some bonds don't break;
they simply rest,
and come back sweeter,
like a reprise the heart wasn't done hearing.

So tonight the percussion section rises for her
playing to the click of her stilettos,
the boom of hips that keep perfect time,
the rhythm of a woman who knows her worth
and never drops the beat.

We salute her
the Queen in rainbow outfits and heels,
the nurse, the mother, the maker,
the warrior with a needle in her hand
and healing in her spirit,
the friend who stands center-stage
without ever asking for the spotlight.

To my Sister,
my day one,
my forever melody…

You are still caking,
still radiating,
still here,
still miraculous.

And I'm still
calling you
Queen.

The R&B Singer

When the horns lifted,
he entered like a crescendo
smooth,
composed,
a man who carried silence
the way other men carried swagger.

He didn't walk into rooms.
He arrived,
the way R&B does—
slow burn,
low light,
something warm gathering in the chest
before the first note lands.

Back then,
I was still finding the shape of my own shine,
but he saw the music in me
before I heard it myself.

He moved with that velvet confidence
the old groups had.
Troop,
Jodeci,
Maxwell-in-the-blue-light energy
with height and harmony,
a quiet storm wrapped in a gentleman's frame.

And when he spoke,
my name became melody.

"Baby girl"
wasn't a phrase
it was an octave.

A soft, secret key
that opened something ancient
and tender
in me.

That night,
his presence felt like a song
that had waited decades to be written
a track meant to play only
when the timing
was finally ripe.

With him,
I never folded inward.
I never dimmed.
I never guessed.
I stood beside him
the way a harmony stands beside a lead
not competing,
just beautifully aligned.

Our connection was never chaos.
Never crowded.
Never demanding a definition.
It was a composition
a quiet covenant
of ease,
respect,
and gentle remembering.

Even now,
the melody hasn't faded.
It sings in the soft places.
It drifts through memory
like a hook you never get tired of
familiar,
soothing,
timeless.

He was not a chapter.
He was a chord.
A steady one
deep as bass,
smooth as tenor,
sweet as falsetto.

An anchor
in a world full of noise.
A velvet harmony
I can still hear
when the room goes quiet.
My R&B Singer.

The melody that never missed a note.
The song the universe wrote for me
before I knew
I needed music.

The Harp Seduction

She blushes like moonlight meeting its own reflection,
as if unaware of the galaxies pulsing beneath her skin.
But she knows.
She always knows.

Each string she touches echoes her name in secret,
a rhythm stitched from bone and starlight,
from the women who learned how to sing
without ever being heard.

Her fingers move like memory,
like prophecy dressed in gold.
Every note, an ache,
every pause, a choice.

She plays him gently at first,
testing his breath against her tempo.
Then the fire comes
low, deliberate, fearless.
She weaves him into her bass line,
decides what part of him belongs in her song.

For some, she offers sweetness
a melody of mercy and silk.
For others, something deeper
a cadence that consumes.

The harp curves like her body,
full of secrets and sacred geometry.
Her hands are anointed in candied light,
her lashes dusted with cosmic shimmer.

When she plays,
the room forgets its name.

This is not performance.
This is invocation.
This is power disguised as grace
the art of becoming sound itself.

She is the storm behind stillness,
the muse and the mortal,
the prayer and the sin.

And when the music ends,
the silence trembles
because it remembers her.

Midnight Gospel

There was a way that she moved
that made the bass stand still.
Hips baptized in rhythm,
arms whispering scripture to the smoke.

The jukebox groaned out a sermon,
each note thick as molasses,
and she answered with her body
slow, certain,
like she knew the language of thunder.

Sweat shimmered on her collarbone,
a congregation of eyes caught between prayer and sin.
Someone whispered, Lord, have mercy,
but mercy had already slipped out the back door.

This was not a dance.
It was deliverance.
It was the gospel of woman,
sovereign and uncontained.

Her heels struck the floor like drums
calling the ancestors from sleep.
And suddenly, the juke joint turned to forest
saxophones became cicadas,
ceiling lights flickered into stars.

The night remembered its rhythm.

She was every woman who'd ever been told to be quiet,
answering back with her hips,

her shoulders,
her sacred sway.

And when she stopped,
the silence bowed its head.

Because every soul in that room
had just been to church
the kind that starts in a juke joint
and ends somewhere near heaven.

Trumpet Heart

Time paused the day I met him
a boy with music folded behind his smile,
a sound too tender to name.

His laughter—clean, unchained
rose through humid air
like brass catching sunlight.

The way he moved,
confident, calm,
felt like rhythm before the beat.

He was melody before memory formed,
a vibration beneath my ribs,
a northern wind finding home in southern heat.

When silence filled my world,
he stayed
not to fix it,
but to remind me what stillness could hold.

There are some songs
you never outgrow
only whisper softer over time.

The trumpet called that night
notes smooth and alive,
a sound stitched with joy and promise.

I remember the light in his eyes
steady, sincere,

a kind of peace I didn't yet have words for.

Years drifted
and still, when I hear that tone,
the air leans back in recognition.

Not longing.
Not loss.

Just the quiet gratitude
for a boy who gave me gentleness
before the world demanded strength.

Because some souls
never leave your rhythm
they just live quieter
in the harmony between heartbeats.

And when the horn moans low,
I feel it again
the kindness,
the laughter,
the music that made me believe
in joy again.

He was the first song,
the golden note I still remember
and somewhere,
beneath the hush of time,
the trumpet still remembers my name.

The Opera Singer

She stood center stage,
bathed in gold and ghosts,
where silence bowed before her breath.
The velvet curtains trembled
a prelude.

A single light found her cheekbone
and crowned it in tremor and truth.

Her gown carried storms in its folds,
lace stitched with the memory of every woman
who sang through sorrow and still sounded like joy.

When she inhaled, the air changed keys.
When she exhaled,
the violins in heaven tightened their strings.

The first note rose
soft, deliberate, dangerous
a pulse that rippled through pews and pewter,
through cracked stained glass and rib cages.

Her vibrato was thunder with perfect pitch,
her range a confession between God and grief.
The audience leaned in,
not to hear her
but to be forgiven.

Each chord climbed like smoke
toward the rafters of forever.

Each note—a prayer resurrected
from the bones of those who hummed before her.

Her song bent time,
turned mourning into movement,
shattered marble with mercy.

Oceans rose to meet her frequency,
clouds rearranged their rhythm,
and the moon swayed in tempo with her breath.

The angels whispered,
She sings in the language of becoming.

Her final note lingered …

half-lullaby, half-battle cry
echoing through the ribs of the world.
When it broke,
the sky cracked open with applause.

And when silence returned,
it wasn't empty
it was reverent.

Because somewhere between E-flat and eternity,
a Black woman taught the universe
how to feel again.

The Cigar Bar

He was my first doorway
into a world stitched in velvet and altitude
penthouse skies, piano keys glowing under city light,
and the kind of service where a man would nod once and say,
"She's with me. Give her whatever she wants."

There was a storm living inside that gentleness,
a quiet thunder.

He wore it the way some men wear watches
effortlessly,
intentionally,
like power was just a part of the outfit.

A suit coat draped over broad shoulders,
shades that hid what he felt,
and a slow, indulgent drag of a cigar
that filled the room with a dark, smoky promise
bass notes curling through the air,
rich and deliberate.

Kentucky lived in him
not the place,
the *build* of it.

That steadfast, stallion-strong presence
that makes you wonder
what the land must have shaped in him
for him to stand so certain.

Younger, soft, naïve,
still arriving into my own shine.

But he…
he had a way of lifting the veil on luxury,
placing me at tables I'd only dreamed about,
letting me taste a world
where ease was expected
and opulence was casual.

He didn't talk much.
He didn't need to.

His silence was a room,
and I learned how to breathe differently inside it
to hear the low hum beneath his presence,
the unspoken rhythm
that made the night feel scored.

I can still feel the piano notes from that night,
the way the air vibrated around us,
how the short hair I wear now
the very cut he said would drive him wild
has become its own kind of legacy,
a quiet symphony of memory and arrival,
a reminder of the girl I was
and the woman I've grown into.

He was a moment
that stretched itself into memory,
and a memory that softened into myth.

A quiet storm
that didn't claim me
just marked me,
with an experience
that still lives
in the soft chambers
of my eternity.

ENCORE II: The Lineage & The Legacy

Ancestral· Grounded · Triumphant

The Band Section

They walk in like a bassline
steady, sure,
a rhythm the world didn't teach them,
but one they mastered anyway

Black men.
Southern men.
Men who press their pants
before they press their point.
Men whose cologne hits the room
five seconds before they do
not loud, just announcing
that excellence has arrived
in a key all of their own.

In the band section,
their confidence warms the air
like a horn warming up
not rushed, not loud,
just present.

Just that state-of-mind sexy
that ain't got nothing to do
with age,
or abs,
or angles
but everything to do
with spirit.

These are the brothers
the news won't tell you about,

the ones who survived systems
designed to quiet their shine.

The ones who still show up
as fathers, husbands,
protectors, friends,
the men who hold the world together
without applause,
without credit,
without complaint.

Look at them
in fresh cuts, bald heads gleaming,
waves on swim,
dreads tightened with care,
braids that tell stories.

Linen suits catching the wind,
hard-bottom shoes tapping out a rhythm
older than the blues
and smoother than Sunday morning.

These are the men
who smell like legacy
like oak and bourbon,
like barbershop laughter,
like somebody raised them
right.

In the band section,
they don't just look good
they **sound** good.

Voices deep like timpani,
wisdom humming at the bottom
of every sentence.

You can hear their whole lineage
in a single
"Hey, sweetheart."

And Black men of the South
oh, they got a distinct vibration.

Respectful nods.
Hats tipped.
Handshakes firm enough to
restore your faith
in being held.

This is for the men
who carry joy like a drumbeat,
who dance after being bruised
by a world that mistakes survival
for aggression.

For the men who love Black women
out loud,
who show up clean, ready, steady
in the choir stand of life,
in the juke joint of memory,
in the symphony of our community.

To the brothers in the band section:
I see you.

I Love the Music you *make*
just by being Here.

Keep playing …

The World needs
Your *sound*.

Helen's Song

She came into this world
with July heat in her veins
and Charleston salt on her tongue
a girl raised by roses
and rebellion,
born knowing how to make life bend
without ever breaking her.

Her laughter carried thunder.
Her eyes—wild, wide-open fire
held whole universes in their pupils,
the kind of woman whose presence
shifted the air before she spoke.

Red lipstick.
Pressed curls.

A sway in her walk
that dared the world not to look.

She loved love.

Married more than once,
not out of searching
but out of choosing
she was a woman who believed
that joy should return again and again,
each time with a different face
and a fresh bouquet of possibility.

She cussed with purpose,
danced with abandon,
and held court at every gathering
when the music slowed,
she'd shout,
"Turn these lights on
ain't no lovers in here!"
because her spirit refused smallness
or dimmed-down versions of life.

I only had her for a moment,
but a moment with her
was a whole inheritance.

She saw me
not the girl trying to stay small,
not the child learning to survive,
but the woman
with the shine she recognized
because she carried the same flame.

In every photo,
her eyes burn bright
not with sorrow,
but with a hunger for living,
a taste for pleasure,
a knowing that the world
could never take her softness
nor quiet the music in her bones.

Eighty-six years she lived
fierce, fragrant, unforgettable
and the earth is louder

because she passed through it.

This is her song.

A melody stitched in my memory,
a rhythm that lives beneath my ribs,
a legacy of boldness and beauty
that refuses to be forgotten.

She lived. She loved. She danced.

And her music
her wild, laughing music
still *plays* in me.

Josie's Blues

They say the blues was born in Mississippi,
but I swear it found its home
on her sapphire porch
beneath those weeping willows
that bent low just to listen.

Her voice was a drumline
for the whole neighborhood
booming, bold,
brass rising behind her,
laughter shaking the paint
as it slowly peeled from the walls
while hope stood waiting
at the front of the wooden steps.

She sat high in her chair,
wrapped in satin blue.

Her smile sparkled like diamonds
that danced in the sunlight.

Her hair was neatly pressed,
her silver-encrusted shoes catching light
like small miracles.

Bus drivers slowed their wheels just to wave.
Passersby hollered and spoke her name,
and Union Street felt like home.

Her house smelled like warm peach and cinnamon
and second chances

music and mercy simmering
in the same pot.

She took in whoever needed a place, a home,
fed them stories with their supper,
and commanded they hold their heads high
that they were royalty
whether the world agreed or not.

She ruled from her throne by the window
gold lingering across the sill,
her presence loud and loving,
still calling the world by name.

She could move heaven and earth
with the sound of her voice,
and the heavens would bow
to her command.

You could hear her through the curtains
soft, steady
like church and juke joint
meeting halfway.

Now, when the wind moves slow
through Duval nights,
I swear I hear her voice
whisper through the wheels of the train
in the far distance.

And I smile,
because I know

this beautiful sound
is Josie's Blues.

Capricorn Rising

Before she belonged to the world of women,
she belonged to the winter sky
a Capricorn rising in garnet flame,
born under a January moon
that taught its daughters
how to survive the cold
and still shine.

I once imagined her flawless
as if mothers were carved whole,
as if the universe finished them
before placing children in their arms.
But even stars fracture
before they glow.

I built her from longing,
from the soft ache of what I needed,
forgetting she was once a girl
learning how to hold her own light
without burning.

At seventeen, she became a mother.
By twenty, a wife.
A widow at twenty-eight.

Grief draped her shoulders
like a winter shawl
she never learned to take off.

Loss settled into her bones,
taught her to speak in silence,

to dance in survival,
to love in the language
she had been given
sharp, guarded,
half-snow, half-flame.

There were days her love cut cold.
Days her storms echoed loud.
I became the child
who learned to read her atmosphere
tracking the weather in her voice,
folding myself small
to keep the house from breaking.

Between her laughter and her rage,
I learned to shrink,
to adjust my shape
to fit inside her shadow.

I carried her pain like a second skin,
not knowing it wasn't mine to hold.

Sometimes I felt her envy
the sting of watching me bloom
in places she never got to grow.

Capricorn women
are not jealous by accident;
they ache for what the world stole
before they had language for loss.

I didn't understand then
that exhaustion can shimmer like garnet,

Red lipstick can armor a battlefield,
and a woman can turn her pain
into a quiet prayer
and still step out the door
radiant,
as if the sun rose just to follow her.

She was regal
in the way mountains are regal
unyielding,
weathered,
beautiful because they survive
what would break anything else.

Her love was complicated,
sometimes wounding,
but it was the only music
she had ever been taught.

I no longer silence what it carved in me
the ache,
the intuition,
the way my body learned to brace.
But honoring her
does not mean erasing the truth.

It means naming both
the bruise and the brilliance,
the storm and the crown.
It means surviving,
and choosing softness anyway.

Now I honor her differently
for the beauty she refused to bury,
for the fire she carried alone,
for the lessons she never meant
but still left glowing inside me.

Because before she was my mother,
she was a garnet-born girl
learning to stand on a spinning earth,
steadying herself with mountain hands
and winter resilience.

And every time I rise
slow, steady, ancient,
garnet in my blood,
light in my spine
I rise in the image
of the Capricorn woman
who came before me,
whose storms shaped my strength,
whose fire began my story,
whose name
the stars whispered first.

Sagittarius Dancer

She is rhythm before music,
a pulse the universe follows
just to keep time.

Fire-sign fingertips
she touches a room
and the air remembers
how to move.

She enters already in motion,
a pivot of hips,
a knowing turn,
the kind of balance that doesn't wobble
because it trusts the floor.

There is discipline in her lines,
truth in her posture.
She holds stillness
the way dancers do
not empty,
but charged.

When she spins,
the wind learns her name.
When she stops,
the room exhales.

Grace lives in her ankles.
Precision in her spine.
Joy breaks loose
when she lets the fire show.

She dances like a woman
who understands timing
when to leap,
when to hold the pose,
when to land without apology.

She is truth
spoken with hips,
correction wrapped in laughter,
the mirror that doesn't soften
what you need to see
to grow.

Her spirit cuts clean
Sagittarius straight-shot fire,
arrowed honesty,
unfiltered,
undeniable.

We met in the place
where sisterhood is chosen,
not inherited—
a constellation shaped like two women
who refuse to break form.

She is the arrow.
I am the flame.

And God,
the great choreographer,
threaded our names
through the same silver sky,

counting us in
before we ever knew the steps.

Some souls arrive as dancers.
Some as teachers.
Some as fire.

She came as all three.

And my life
has never stopped moving
since.

Four Part Harmony

We were a harmony
before we knew what the word meant
four girls with red lipstick,
Olan Mills smiles,
and confidence we borrowed from R&B divas
who taught us how to hold our own light.
and catch the beat
without missing a step.

Back then,
we thought the world was something
you stepped into wearing matching colors
and shoulder-to-shoulder loyalty
soft, fierce, unbreakable,
like the opening note of a girl-group anthem
we didn't yet know we were singing.

But growing up
is its own kind of tour.

We loved, lost, married, divorced—
raised babies,
raised hell,
and raised ourselves
into women we didn't know
we were becoming.

Still
the harmony never changed.
We remained a four-girl group
long after the photo faded.

Friendship like ours doesn't disappear
it deepens,
dropping into a lower octave
only time can teach.

Now we laugh different.
We love harder.
We show up softer
because we know what survival costs
and what sisterhood gives back.

We've held secrets,
held babies,
held each other
when the world got too loud,
when life went off-key,
one of us needed the others
to *sang* the tune back into her bones.

And through every decade,
every season that tried to redesign us,
the truth stayed the same

We were magic then.
We are magic now.
And the universe still knows our blend
when it hears it
that unmistakable harmony
only four hearts can make.

Thirty years in,
we are still that girl group
still harmonizing,

still glowing,
still holding on to the kind of love
that never falls out of tune.

Emerald Frequency

She came into this world
tuned to a different wavelength
an emerald frequency
the universe forgot to explain to us,
but whispered directly into her bones
like a secret note
in a symphony only she could hear.

Five feet of fire.
Ninety-five pounds of spark.
A girl wrapped in green light,
living in a rhythm all her own.
a tempo unteachable,
a melody untouched.

Before we knew the language for it,
they called her broken.
They drew charts and labels.
They measured what she wasn't.
But she never asked to be understood
she simply was.

And we
the world around her
were the ones who had to learn
how to listen.

How to hear the soft percussion
beneath her laughter,
the high notes threaded through her joy,

the wild improvisation
in the way she moved through the world.

She didn't come here to adjust.
We adjusted to her.
Her joy demanded it.
Her storms required it.
Her truth insisted on it.

There is something fearless
about a soul who never learned
to dim herself
for the comfort of others.

Something sacred
about a girl who plays,
laughs,
moves,
speaks
in a cadence untouched by shame
a soloist
unbothered by the audience.

She lives unfiltered
a purity the world rarely sees,
a softness forged into stubborn flame,
a spirit the earth could not tame.

We grew up learning her world
bending, shifting, translating,
carrying truths too heavy
for our small hands,
loving her through confusion,

protecting her from cruelty,
figuring out how to hold a sister
who floated where we walked
more stardust than footsteps,
more chorus than body.

There was a moment
I tried to gather her into my orbit
thinking my gravity
could steady her stars.

But even emerald light
has its own direction,
its own sky to travel,
its own rhythm written
in a language older than expectation,
older than instruction,
older than us.

And when I rise
unburdened,
unguarded,
full of love
I rise knowing
her light and mine
were never meant to be carried
only witnessed,
only honored,
only allowed to shine
in the way the universe made them.

Because she is not fragile.

She is not lacking.
She is not less.

She is a color the universe invented
to remind us
that not all brilliance looks the same,
that not all souls arrive polished,
that some light enters the world
through a different door.
an unexpected chord
that still belongs in the score.

She is emerald
rare,
wild,
unyielding,
unbroken.

A small woman
with a universe-sized spirit,
vibrating at a pitch
all her own
a quiet maestro
of her own existence.

And when I rise
through truth,
through tenderness,
through love

I rise knowing
she, too,
is part of my constellation.

My Sister.
My lesson.
My green flame.

My **Emerald Frequency**.

Moonchild

He was born under a stubborn moon
the kind that will not dim,
when the world tries to eclipse it.

A quiet brilliance.
A restless spirit.
A soul stitched together
with constellations he never asked for
and storms he never explained.

They saw the chaos.
I saw the light leaking through it.

He has always been a Moonchild
half-shadow,
half-shimmer,
carrying constellations in the places
he thought were empty.

Brilliant without trying.
Creative without permission.
A mind that operates at frequencies
the ordinary can't hear.
A heart that loves loud,
when the world whispers too soft.

Life handed him labyrinths
twisted paths,
abrupt endings,
beginnings that took more than they gave.
But in the darkest chapters,

he learned how to glow
without guidance.

His laughter is wild starfire,
his dreams heavy with planets
he still wants to build.
He loves in a way that cracks open air,
messy, honest, alive
the kind of love you can only give
when you've seen the underbelly of life
and chose to keep breathing anyway.

They call him dramatic.
I call him cosmic.

They call him lost.
I call him orbiting
trying to find the right sky
to call home.

He bears brilliance like burden,
hurt like history,
and still
beneath it all
is a boy who wanted to shine
without being punished for it.

I have left him
and returned to him
like the moon leaves the morning.
And every time I look at him,
I see the glow still burning.

Because Moonchildren don't break
they shift.

They fade, then blaze again.
They change shape
without losing their light.

A man made of phases,
of brilliance misunderstood,
of galaxies unnamed.

And when I rise,
through truth
through tenderness
through legacy
I rise knowing
his light is part of my creation story.

He is the Moonchild
and no matter how far he drifts,
he is still made of stars
that remember their way home.

Jade Couture
Joy in the Heavens

She left the earth
the way a star slips from the sky
quiet to the eye,
but loud to the soul.

Her spirit rose in lavender light,
a soft-burning flame
with the attitude of a woman
who never learned to whisper her truth.

I feel the shape of her laughter
wild, sharp, honey-sweet at the edges
the kind that could slice through delusion
and still leave a blessing behind.

She was the kind of woman
whose honesty wore hoop earrings,
whose love walked barefoot through fire
and didn't lose its color.

When she spoke,
the room shifted keys.
When she left,
the universe created a new octave
to hold her name.

Now she lives in frequencies
in the purple warmth of twilight,
in the gold hush before sunrise,
in the celestial quiet

of a truth-teller who earned her wings
long before she ever needed them.

Sometimes
I swear I feel her beside me
not as memory,
but as music.

A bassline of warning:
don't shrink.
A treble note of tenderness:
you are more than you know.
A whispered chord of love:
I'm still here.

Her energy never died.
It transformed
into a constellation with attitude,
a soft guardian with sharp edges,
a star that talks back.

Joy is not gone.
She's ascended
a celestial woman
braiding heaven into my steps,
lighting the air around my grief,
turning my sorrow
into something shimmering.

She is purple flame.
She is cosmic truth.
She is laughter that refuses extinction.
She is the star

that spells my name
every time I forget
I am worthy of light.

Joy in the heavens
the friend who became
a forever frequency.

The Go-Go Band

They don't walk into the room
they enter on the one,
on the beat,
on that signature DMV sway
you can spot from across the Potomac.

Black men from D.C., Maryland, Virginia...
baby, that's a different frequency.
A whole different tempo.
A vibration you feel in your knees
before you feel it in your chest.

These are the men
who carry rhythm in their bloodline,
swagger in their bones,
and patience only for
the women, the work,
and the ancestors watching.

They stand like a drum line
shoulders relaxed,
eyes observant,
hands ready,
knowing damn well
they are the pulse
of wherever they stand.

Dreads fresh.
Beards lined to perfection.
White tees crisp.

Nike boots stomped in just right.
That faint scent of shea butter, oud,
and good intentions.

Go-Go men don't just dance
they lead the whole floor.
A shoulder dip here,
a two-step there,
a body roll that whispers,
"I know exactly who I am."

They clap on the upbeat,
nod when the pocket hits,
and grin that slow, dangerous grin
when the congos slide in and say,
"Yeah… this right here."

These are the brothers
who survived the city,
politics,
the targets put on their backs,
the stories nobody tells.
And still
Still—
they show up fly,
intentional,
ready to celebrate joy
like it's a revolutionary act.

In the **Go-Go Band**,
their voices ride the rhythm
deep, gritty, familiar
the kind of tone that could

calm you, claim you,
or call you out
with one word:
"Hey."

They are the spirit of the block cookout,
the sound of U Street at midnight,
the heartbeat of a culture
in constant motion.

To the men of the DMV:
you don't just bring the music
you ARE the music.
The pulse.
The hype.
The grit.
The hometown pride.

You are the reason the floor shakes
and the air gets thick
and the night turns holy.

Keep the beat going.
The world ain't ready
but we stay ready
because you do.

Key Signature in Blue

He arrived like a key signature changing
quiet at first,
just a shift on the page,
a subtle rearranging of sound
I didn't yet know how to name.

Not a hero.
Not a savior.
Not a thunderbolt of fate.

Just a steady note—
clear, dependable,
a Tennessee-blue hum
that softened the dissonance around me.

He didn't rescue me.
He opened a door,
and I stepped out of the noise.

Behind it:
Safety.
A world that bruised less loudly.
A gentler rhythm,
carried easily,
as naturally as breath.

There was a quiet magic to him
not the blazing kind that blinds you,
but the kind that holds.

A Titan heart,
all discipline and direction,
anchoring storms
he never asked to navigate.

He was lean, resolute,
a man carved in clean lines
and untold sacrifice.

He treated my history
like something worth protecting.

He taught me structure.
Rhythm.
The calm between the measures.
The difference between
enduring a life
and living inside one.

Our song wasn't forever
but it was formative.
Foundational.
The kind of movement
that doesn't need a reprise
to remain alive.

Every symphony has a moment
where the music shifts
where the key changes
and the listener sits up,
sensing something new beginning.

He was that moment.

And long after the melody moved on,
I can still hear the note of it
quiet, unwavering,
a small mercy written in blue
that led me back to myself.

ENCORE III: The Lineage & The Legacy

Soft· Incandescent · Otherworldly

Spirits That Travel

Some loves don't stay in the body.
They travel.

Through memory,
through sound,
through the hush between heartbeats
where breath becomes a language,
and the quiet lingers beneath the ribs
turns into music you feel before you hear.

Some spirits know your name
before you ever speak it.

They rise when you rise,
follow you through seasons,
and sit softly beside you
when the world forgets your softness
a low, lingering note
only your soul can recognize.

She loved people
who never really left
not because they held on,
but because the connection
was stitched into the unseen.

A thread.
A pulse.
A recognition.
A chord that keeps vibrating
long after the moment has passed.

The kind of bond
that doesn't beg to be kept
it simply exists.

Alive in the places you've healed,
and in the places
you haven't touched.

There are spirits
that pass through us
like wind through lace curtains
gentle, familiar,
moving the room
the way a soft violin shifts the air.

They remind us that love
is not always meant to stay tethered
to skin and circumstance.

Sometimes it moves freely,
returning only to remind you
that you are still capable
of feeling deeply,
vividly,
dangerously alive.

Not all love is meant to stay.
But some spirits—
they travel with you,
carrying their own quiet melody,
following you from lifetime to lifetime
like a song that refuses to end.

Jamaica Queens

He moved through the world
with the quiet magic
of a man carved from constellations
a man whose spirit shimmered
with that unmistakable
Queens-born glow.

You couldn't pinpoint the moment
he entered her life.
It felt less like an arrival
and more like a shift
as if the air recognized him
before she did,
as if some old knowing
opened its eyes inside her
and whispered,
"Pay attention."

There was something cosmic
in the way he carried himself.

A warmth that wrapped around her
like familiar incense,
like the kind of softness
a woman only encounters
once every few lifetimes.

He didn't touch her
yet she felt him.

A gentle gravity,
a pull made of heat and promise,
drawing her toward a love
that felt both ancient
and brand new.

He spoke,
and the sound lingered in the air
like smoke curled around honey
low, warm,
a vibration more than a voice.
A rhythm that slipped beneath her ribs
and made a home there
without force,
without urgency,
without noise.

His presence moved like moonlight:
slow, deliberate,
a quiet illumination
she couldn't look away from.

He wasn't a storm.
He was the stillness
before the rain.

The warmth after it.
The breath a woman exhales
when she finally feels safe
in the arms of a truth
she didn't have to chase.

And she
she softened in ways
that only destiny can explain.
The kind of softening
that turns a woman luminous,
as if her heart
had finally remembered its song.

When he looked at her,
something magical hung in the moment
not worship,
not possession,
but recognition.

A soul seeing a soul
through the veil of this world
and all the others.

Whatever lived between them
felt threaded by the divine
a quiet golden passage
only they could walk,
where time didn't rush,
and love didn't demand,
and everything glowed
in the color of fate.

He carried the pulse of Queens.
She carried the heat of hope.

And together,
they created a frequency
that felt like homecoming.

Not loud.
Not fast.
Just *eternal*.

Stardust

Before the world named me woman,
I was light.
Uncontained.
Unbothered by gravity.
A pulse wandering the heavens
looking for a body bold enough
to hold me.

I have carried galaxies in my ribs
for longer than memory remembers.

Supernovas slept behind my eyes.
Comets curved at the thought of me.

Stars whispered my name
before I ever learned to breathe it.

Some say we're made of dust
but mine has always shimmered,
knowing it belonged to something
older than science,
truer than fate.

I learned early
that brightness is a kind of burden.

So I dimmed myself
to make the world comfortable
folding constellations small,
tucking brilliance beneath bone,
pretending I was only human.

The universe has a way
of calling its daughters back.

One night
quiet, unremarkable,
ordinary to anyone else
something in me cracked open,
and all the light I'd tucked away
came rushing out
like a thousand suns
escaping a single silence.

I felt the old heat return
the celestial knowing,
the sacred fire
that makes gods out of ordinary things.

My back straightened
like a horizon lifting.
My breath expanded
into whole skies.
My voice found its original pitch
low, ancient, familiar
only to the women who came before me.

Helen hummed through my veins.
Marion stood behind me
like a pillar of starlight.

And every ancestor
whoever loved me
stepped forward
to witness my rising.

I did not *glow*.
I burned
quietly,
precisely,
like a prophecy claiming its shape.

My skin remembered the cosmos
that built it.

My bones loosened their fear.
My spirit took its rightful altitude.

I wasn't reborn.
I was revealed.

And when the night wind touched me,
it whispered only one truth:

Welcome back.
We've been waiting for you.

Because I was never meant to live small,
never meant to forget,
never meant to hide my shine.

I am not dust.
I am not memory.
I am not miracle.

I am Stardust
the kind that knows its own power,
and shines.

The kind that rises
because it was designed
to be seen.

Echoes on the Leaves

As Autumn settles in,
if you listen closely,
you can hear echoes on the leaves
love, fairytales, and promises
rustling beneath the branches
as the season exhales into gold.

The forest still remembers them
the woman with skin like dusk,
the man with laughter deep as thunder.

They met beneath the apricot sky,
where light bent through the trees
and time forgot to move.

She was warmth wrapped in linen,
barefoot and golden at the edges.
He smelled of rain and bourbon,
his smile a storm she didn't fear.

They didn't speak at first
just breathed each other in
as the air around them trembled.

When he touched her wrist,
the leaves began to dance,
a quiet harmony between pulse and wind.

Their bodies found a rhythm
older than language

a melody written before the world had sound.

He kissed her shoulder,
and a thousand petals loosened from the trees.
She whispered his name,
and every root shivered beneath the soil.

The forest leaned closer,
holding its breath for what came next
the way devotion settled softly,
like dusk over water.

The lush of love moved through the hills of the trees,
a silence dressed in matrimony,
where the birds refused to sing
honoring a union too sacred for sound.

Those echoes are of many lovers come and gone,
who found home
in the shadows of the trees.

Pulses of breath
sighs carried through branches,
their touch imprinted on bark,
laughter rustling through time itself.

So when the wind sighs,
you can still hear them
past loves who left pieces of themselves
woven into the earth's soft song,
in hues of gold, red, and orange leaves,
devotion lingering like perfume
on the edge of forever.

Whiskey & Gardenias

I've made peace with my contradictions
the burn and the bloom,
the bite and the beauty.

Whiskey warms my throat,
gardenias crown my wrist.
The room settles low,
and I breathe with it
half prayer, half praise.

My fire's been called too much,
my mood, too quiet,
my rhythm too direct,
my confidence too knowing
because I learned how to quench a flame
with the whisper of my lips,
how to hush desire
without ever raising my voice.

There's art in my restraint,
and poetry in my fearlessness.
Uninhibited. Reckless.
And yes, there's danger in my calm.

I move like confession wrapped in perfume,
glow like sin forgiven.
Cigarettes on the nightstand,
jazz on repeat,
a little lipstick left behind
on the glass and the goodbye.

I pour for peace now,
and mini celebrations
for the nights I stayed soft
and the mornings I chose myself.

The gardenia Queen.
The mystical god.
The mermaid who refused to drown.

I don't chase light anymore
I am it.
Dripping in grace and bourbon,
sweet enough to burn slow,
sacred enough to stay whole.

Because women like me
don't fade
we evolve into flavor.
Into worship.
Into wonder.

When the Willow Swings

Looking through the aquamarine sky,
I felt the glide of her rhythm move through every step
the way she smiled, notes of a flute;
her voice, melody hovering between the air and the wind.

And there she stood — the Willow.

Her skin, deep caramel kissed by light,
strong, grounded in chocolate roots
braided deep in the earth's memory.

Her arms, long branches dressed in silver-green,
flowed like emerald water in a crystal lake
a slow, rhythmic dance of knowing.

As a child, I thought she was sad
her arms hanging low,
the wind weeping through her leaves.

But even then, I felt something deeper
in her quiet bending
the weight of words left unsaid,
the hush of worlds she carried.
Still, she swayed with grace, not grief,
and I didn't yet understand
what it meant to weep and still stand tall.

Summers passed,
and I found her again
the same sway, the same strength,

a woman cloaked in green light.
When I cried, she listened.

When I prayed without words,
she answered with a rustle,
a rhythm only stillness could translate.

Now years later,
I know her not as sorrow,
but as song.
Her movement is music.
Her bending, jazz.
Her silence, symphony.

Because even in her weeping,
she was beautiful.
In her bending,
she was strong.

She is the woman we all come from
rooted, radiant, reaching.

And when the willow swings,
the night listens.

Every leaf carries her survival,
every shadow remembers her prayer.

And now that she rests deep in the earth's core,
I stand beneath her open sky,
my palms lifted, my heart unhidden,
and I whisper back
thank you.

Black Velvet & Rose Gold

They step into the room
like a chord warming up
black velvet, rose gold,
a hush before the first note drops.

Soft
where the world expected steel.
Shining
in the places they tried to dim.

Women with sheet music folded beneath their ribs,
who remember the sound of their own becoming
even when the orchestra falls silent.

Listen
you can hear their entrance
before you ever see them.

A low hum of power,
a shimmer of light on the edge of the stage,
a fire tuning itself in the dark.

Black velvet
the depth, the mystery,
that slow-burn softness
you feel before you understand.

Rose gold
the warmth, the glow,
the bloom that keeps blooming
no matter who tried to bury the root.

They move like a jazz line
unexpected,
unapologetic,
impossible to imitate.

Women wrapped in night
and lit from within,
commanding the room
with a presence that bends the air.

And anyone who has ever loved them
or lost them
knows the truth:

You cannot dim a woman
who was born from music and light.

She rises
every time
in black velvet and rose gold,
conducting her own radiant return.

Marshmallow Clouds

The bells tolled somewhere
far out in the Atlantic
a sound the ocean carried
like a secret meant only for her.

Perched on a lone warm rock,
she waited.
Not for rescue
but for the moment the sky
remembered her name.

As the sun bowed low
and the first stars assembled,
she rose
a mermaid slipping out of seafoam
and into evening's veil.

The clouds opened for her
like a soft invitation.
She stepped onto them gently,
careful not to break through
their marshmallow hush ...
the sky humming a quiet melody
only her spirit could hear.

She reached for a star,
held it like a ripe peach,
kissed it with the memory of an old love
a slow, lingering press of lips
and bit into its golden flesh...

Gentle,
the way one bites a lover's bottom lip
when desire remembers itself.

The galaxy brightened at her touch,
scattering gold in every direction
as if blessing the heart she loved
across impossible miles.

Up, up she climbed,
each cloud a rung
on the ladder to him.

And when she reached the place
where his spirit lived
in the folds of the night sky,
she curled beside him
her breath settling into his,
her dreams resting in the warm outline
of his silhouette.

She stayed there until dawn,
wrapped in the hush
of love the world could not explain.

And when the morning sun rose
calling her back to the waves
she descended the sky
one soft cloud at a time,
returning to the ocean
with stardust still glowing
on her lips.

INTERMISSION III — The Rose Garden

The Rose Garden:
When He Returned to the Sky: Intermission

The air moved like a prelude
Champney Pink and Noisette braided
into one slow, waiting breath.
Paris leaning into Charleston.
Petals holding time
in a sustained note
the garden had been rehearsing
for generations.

I entered barefoot,
perfumed with gardenia,
red on my toes like a quiet drum signal.
Couture peach whispering around my legs
in a hush of taffeta and intention.
Aquamarine rang soft at my throat,
echoed in my ears,
kept time at my wrists
a private orchestra of light.

The sun lowered itself
in ritardando,
gold stretching into amber,
as if the sky knew
this was not a moment
for sharp endings.

Then...
a new instrument entered the score.

His presence arrived
before his body did.

A steady baritone of stature.
Calm in a tailored register.

Six-foot-three of grounded rhythm,
hair rising in quiet crescents of curl,
eyes carrying that familiar
major-and-minor depth.

And when he smiled,
that small diamond gap
caught the last clean note of daylight
and rang it outward.

I stood on instinct.
The music in me already rising
to meet the key, it recognized.

When he gathered me into his arms,
the distance of lifetimes
resolved into harmony.
Not ache
recognition.
Not longing
arrival.
Eight thousand years
folded into a single, settled chord.

We sat on the bench
as the sun completed its final measure.

Our conversation moved
in unhurried phrasing
resting where it belonged,
no rushing the tempo,
no fear of silence between notes.

The roses kept counterpoint.
The sky held the sustain.

When it was time,
his goodbye entered
in a softer key
no heaviness,
no dragging diminuendo,
only fullness,
only completion.

As he moved farther away,
he paused beneath the magnolia tree
at the edge of the garden
its wide leaves holding the evening
like a quiet shield.

Then he lifted from the garden
the way melody lifts from breath
light loosening into cloud,
presence thinning into promise,
the final note completing itself
as he returned to the sky.

When the last vibration
settled back into stillness,
standing alone

in a garden still warm with roses, magnolia, and echo,
the truth arrived on its own low note:

I was never alone.

FINAL CURTAIN: Marion Alexander Cafe

Haitian· Charleston · Eternal

Marion Alexander Café

There's a place in Charleston
where the air tastes like ancestry
espresso, brass, and jasmine.
Roses climb the brick like memory,
their petals whispering *__Noisette__* in French tones.

Inside, the tables gleam mahogany and salt.
The barista hums a Creole hymn under her breath.
And every cup carries a lineage
Marion's patience, Alexander's promise,
the sweet persistence of men who built things
from soil and silence.

Steam lifts like prayer from porcelain lips.
Gold spoons chime against china
in soft, ancestral applause.
Somewhere in the back,
a radio croons an old love backward through time
as the windows listens.

I stir sugar into my coffee
and taste the generations
Haitian thunder, Lowcountry rain,
the hum of a saxophone across the bay.
Every sip a prayer,
every pour a return home.

Outside, the street moves on
tourists laughing, horses clicking history forward,
the city dressed in its Sunday bones.
But in here, time loosens its grip.

In here, the past sits down beside me
and orders something warm.

This is where I write my legacy.
Between sips, between songs
where roots meet rhythm
and daughters remember their bloom.

Where names once whispered
become signatures.

Where survival softens into sweetness.

Where what was carried quietly
is finally allowed to be seen.

Because somewhere between the rose and the roast,
we become our ancestors' encore.

And the music doesn't end
it just learns how to breathe through us.

Notes in Blue

The blues was born
on nights like this,
when sorrow learned how to hum
so it wouldn't scream.

Born from Black hands
holding absence.
From women singing prayers
into cotton and steam.
From men whose names
became echoes
instead of footsteps,
portraits instead of presence,
chants instead of goodbyes.

Born from knees on pavement,
from streets turned sanctuaries,
from voices hoarse with truth
still rising anyway.

We only wanted
what grows slow and holy:
Sunday light,
unbroken dancing,
names written
in love's ink
instead of chalk and grief.

We wanted basslines,
not gunfire.
Brass, not sirens.

Songs that finished themselves
without interruption
or apology.

But the night kept interrupting us.

Turning breath into verses.
Turning joy into rehearsal.
Turning bodies into cautionary notes
in a system too large to feel us,
too practiced to stop.

Still...

we marched.
We sang.
We lifted fists and tambourines,
turned sidewalks into choirs,
turned sorrow into sound
the way our ancestors taught us.

We played anyway.

We hummed anyway.

We survived the measure
and refused the silence.

Because we are
the ache
and the brilliance.
The blues **and** the breakthrough.
The sorrow

that learned how to sing
and taught the world to listen.

We are the note
that will not die.
The harmony that outlived the harm.
The sound that kept time
when the clock was against us.

And now
hear us.

Hear the laughter woven through grief.
Hear the joy rising in defiance.
Hear the pride of a people
still standing,
still breathing,
still playing.

This is not mourning music.

This is survival in sound.
This is lineage clapping back.
This is the house lights rising
on a people who endured
and stayed magnificent.

So, Stand.

Clap until your palms ache.
Shout until your chest opens.
Cry if you must.

Laugh if it comes.
Because the blues didn't break us.
It crowned us.

And the music…
the Music
is *still* Playing.

Standing Ovation

For the little Black girl dancing beneath the stars,
the Prom Queen who never got her flowers,
the Valedictorian who entered a world of survival,
the Sisters of the Greek letters who carved open doors,
the Sisters, Wives, Mothers...
the Aunties who kept us together,
the Grandmothers whose stories were stolen,
the Queen.

Queen ...
the orchestra realigns itself
the moment your spirit enters the room.

Strings lean forward,
horns rise to attention,
percussion steadies its heartbeat
because your presence
is its own overture.

Pressed hair gleaming like warm vinyl,
hot comb sizzle lifting into the air
like the first note of a love song.
Silk gowns gliding like moonbeams on marble,
lace fronts laid with precision,
natural coils conducting galaxies,
beaded necklaces and diamond royals
catching light like chandeliers learning to breathe.

You are music,
every inch of you in perfect rhythm:

lashes fluttering like soft cymbals,
full lips glossed in sweet crescendo,
hips swaying to a drum older than time,
cheekbones sculpted like rising notes,
deep-set eyes holding the hush
before a solo that changes everything.

Queen—
Your heart is the choir.

It is the little Black girl
dancing in the shadows of twinkling stars,
waiting for a world gentle enough
to cradle her brilliance.

It is the Prom **Queen**
who never got her flowers
but still found a way
to bloom anyway.

It is the Valedictorian
who walked off the stage
and into a battlefield of survival
with nothing but intelligence, grace,
and a God-touched determination.

It is the Sister in Greek letters,
crossing burning sands
to build legacy and access
where none existed before.

It is the Sister, the Wife, the Mother
loving whole nations from scratch,

praying futures into existence,
holding families together with tired hands
and still finding room
to laugh, to teach, to glow.

For the Aunties who raised us,
and wisdom tucked in every sigh,
who showed up
when nobody else did,
and taught us how to laugh loudly,
dress sharp,
speak truth,
and never dim for anybody.

The ones with peppermints in their purse
and love strong enough
to feel like another mother.
We see you; we thank you; we bow to you.

And for the Grandmothers
the ones whose stories were stolen,
sold, silenced, or buried in whispers,
whose brilliance was disguised as duty,
whose softness was wrapped in survival
we honor you.

We are your wildest dreams walking,
your unfinished sentences given breath,
your prayers wearing perfume and purpose.

Queen
you are the original conductor,
the keeper of rhythm,
the architect of resilience,
the one who taught creation
how to keep time.

Every time you bent but didn't break
A cello found its hum.
Every time you stretch a dollar
into destiny
a bass line deepened.
Every time you lift someone
who had nothing left …
the choir swelled.

Tonight
as the final curtain gathers itself,
as the galaxy holds its breath,
as this book closes its last sacred page
hear this:

The universe is on its feet for you.
The ancestors sway in your honor.
Every instrument bows in reverence.
Every star takes its cue from your light.

Take your place at center stage.

Gather your crown.

Collect your flowers
all of them.

Standing Ovation, **Queen**.

For your *Music*.

For your *Magic*.

For your **Eternal, Incomparable Black** Womanhood.

CURTAIN CALL:
The Women Crowned in Light

They emerge... not from the wings,
but from the galaxies that raised you.
From the hush between heartbeat and hope.
From the shimmering threshold
where memory becomes magic.

They come adorned
in braids, in silvered crowns, in soft brown thunder.
Their gowns whisper like constellations.
their footsteps bloom like midnight jasmine.

These are the women
who held the rhythm when the sky went silent.
The women who guarded the glow
you nearly abandoned.
The women whose laughter shaped your breath
and whose prayers stitched gold
into the torn edges of your becoming.

They take their place at center stage,
not as performers
but as sovereigns.

No rush.
No bow.
Just presence.
Just power.
Just the quiet rule of women
who have carried entire worlds
without ever setting them down.

The air itself straightens in their honor.
The audience rises without command.

This
this is their curtain call.

A coronation in real time.
A lineage made visible.
A chorus of women crowned in light.

FINAL BOW:
The Conductor in Her Own Moonlight

And then the spotlight shifts
slow, deliberate, reverent
to you.

The conductor.
The architect of peach and pulse.
The woman who dared to arrange her scars
into a score
and call it a symphony.

You step forward, regal in your own radiance
not gilded by the world,
but glowing from a fire it could not extinguish.

The stage bends softly beneath your feet.
The velvet air waits in recognition.

You bow,
not out of modesty,
but mastery.
A bow that says:
I rose anyway.
A bow that says:
This glow is inherited, earned, and eternal.

A bow that gathers every woman before you
and every woman after you
into a single, unbreakable note.

The room exhales.
And in that breath,
the universe calls your name
with the tone of prophecy.

HOUSE LIGHTS:
A Benediction

Go now, beloved
but go crowned.

May softness follow your steps
like a loyal wind.
May abundance curl itself at your feet
like warm silk.
May every boundary you draw
become a spell of protection and peace.

May your mornings arrive with gold in their mouth.
May your nights cradle you in velvet hush.
May the ancestors tip their lamps toward your path
each time your hope flickers.

Carry this symphony in your bloodstream.
Let it rise in you whenever the world grows dim.
Let it remind you that you are not merely a witness to beauty
you are the source of it.

When life asks who you are,
lift your chin,
square your shoulders,
and declare without trembling:

I am the glow and the garden.
I am the storm and the softening.
I am the woman who conducts her own becoming.

The lights rise.
The doors open.
The world waits.

Go forth
enchanted, enthroned,
and utterly unforgettable.

A Final Note

May you close this book
feeling a little warmer,
a little lighter,
a little more enchanted
by your own existence.

I hope you walk away humming something new,
moving slower when it matters,
laughing louder when it doesn't.

May you flirt with beauty
and let it flirt back.
May you fall in love with moments again —
with sound, with bodies, with possibility.

Thank you for listening.
Thank you for feeling.
Thank you for being here for the music.

With Light, Love & Wonder …

~ Christina

About the Author

Christina Victoria is an author, publisher, creative visionary, and founder of **Marion Alexander Press**, a boutique publishing house rooted in lineage, artistry, and legacy. She is also the creator of the lifestyle brand **Christina Victoria Collective**, where literature, beauty, and soulful living meet.

Her work centers on empowerment, self-discovery, and reclaiming personal power—inviting women to return to themselves with softness, truth, and fire.

Christina is the author of **Freedom Passage**, a memoir told through intimate letters of healing and reclamation; **The Glow Chronicles**, a devotional for women learning to hear their own voice again; and **The Peach Symphony**, a lush poetic celebration of lineage, sensuality, Southern memory, and divine feminine glow.

Her writing blends **music, ancestry, spirituality, sensuality, and Southern storytelling**, creating a body of work that feels both tender and cinematic, ancestral yet modern, grounded yet otherworldly.

When she's not writing, Christina is building her publishing house, expanding her lifestyle brand, crafting immersive reader experiences, and creating beauty through candles, coffee, and curated visuals that honor her lineage.

She loves flowers, luxurious mornings, soulful music, and candid conversations that make women feel deeply seen.

Through every venture, Christina reminds us of one truth:
It is never too late to return to yourself ... and bloom.

www.ingramcontent.com/pod-product-compliance
Lightning Source LLC
Chambersburg PA
CBHW070703130626
46553CB00005B/1823